CHRISTIANITY IN ROMAN TIMES

Christianity came to Britain in Roman times. Tertullian (*c.* A.D. 200) and Origen (*c.* A.D. 240) refer to British Christianity; in 314 bishops from York, London, and possibly Lincoln, attended a Council at Arles (France), capital of the Roman province to which Britain was attached. Late fourth-century archaeological evidence reveals strong concentrations of Christian remains in some localities, especially around Carlisle, in South Wales, Cornwall, Dorset and Kent.

At first, Christians met in private houses, following New Testament tradition. After the Emperor Constantine's conversion about 312, special centres of worship could be created without fear of persecution. In Britain these took three main forms.

First, Christian urban groups or *ecclesiae* aimed to build and finance churches with attached dwellings for the bishop and clergy. Examples are at Canterbury (the present cathedral site); Colchester (possibly St. Martin's); Lincoln; St. Albans; and Richborough. Some town churches stood in the forum or market place.

After 323, another type appeared outside towns in conventi marked   or lay peop...   ...began as wooden oratories later replaced by rectangular stone buildings, whose altar, on a raised platform, stood near the special burial, later regarded as a shrine. Examples are at Canterbury (St. Martin); Colchester (three buildings later destroyed); London (St. Bride's, Fleet Street, and St. Andrew's, Holborn); St. Albans (near the cathedral and at Verulam Hills Field). The word 'church' derives from *cirice*, a burial ground, from West German *kîrika*, and the Greek *kuriakón* = the Lord's (house), and was not used exclusively in Britain for the building until the tenth century.

Thirdly, there were private churches for public worship on rural estates, usually founded in villas as at Lullingstone, Kent, where excavation revealed fourth-century plaster from an upper room, painted with Christian symbols and praying figures. House churches existed at Frampton and Hinton St. Mary, Dorset; Little Cote, Wiltshire; and elsewhere. At Chedworth, Gloucestershire, the villa's pagan sacred pool was later consecrated, perhaps for baptism.

CHRISTIAN WORSHIP: its basis and setting

The word church has now two meanings: the community of worshipping Christians (formerly called the *ecclesia*), which undertakes, however imperfectly, the role of Christ's body in the world; and the building used regularly for worship.

Membership depends on two sacraments, each an outward and visible sign of an inward and spiritual grace, and each performed in obedience to Christ's commands, well documented in the New Testament.

Baptism, admitting to membership, symbolises the washing away of original, or birth, sin (the human tendency to wrong-doing) and re-birth in the body of Christ, and involves vows of life-long allegiance to Christ after instruction. In early times baptism was usually by complete immersion. Afterwards, the local bishop, representing the whole church, anointed each with chrism (consecrated oil) in confirmation of the candidate's commitment and in the assurance of the strengthening power of God's Holy Spirit in the undertaking.

Baptism took place on Easter Eve, enabling the neophytes (or newly baptised), in white robes, to attend the full Eucharist (*eucharistia*, thanksgiving) for the first time next day, making their communion with the living Christ on the special day celebrating his Resurrection from the dead.

From the first, the Lord's Supper or Eucharist has been celebrated each Sunday and on other special occasions. It involves the blessing and distribution of bread and wine for those present to eat and drink in obedience to Jesus' command at the Last Supper with his disciples on the night before his Crucifixion. He took bread and broke it and gave it to them, saying: 'Take, eat, this is my body which is given for you. Do this, in remembrance of me'; and after supper, he took the cup; and, when he had given thanks, he gave it to them, saying, 'Drink, all, of this, for this is my blood of the new covenant, which is shed for you and for many, for the remission of sins. Do this, as often as you drink it, in remembrance of me'. The new covenant, or new testament, is the contract between God and humanity, offering redemption (Latin, *redemptio*, a buying back) or reconciliation to all estranged from their maker by sin.

Christianity is rooted in Judaism for Jesus was a Jew. Its forms of worship owe much to synagogue services; and daily prayer and Bible reading are expected of Christians.

Its basic moral code has always been the Ten Commandments (Exodus 20: 2–17), whose principles Jesus summed up in the words: 'The Lord our God is one Lord: and thou shalt love the Lord thy God, with all thy heart, and with all thy soul, and with all thy strength: this is the first commandment. And the second is like, namely this, Thou shalt love thy neighbour as thyself. There is no other commandment greater than these. On these two commandments hang all the Law and the Prophets' (Mark 12: 29–31, quoting Deuteronomy 6: 4).

Christ's teaching, therefore, involves care for children, the sick, needy and bereaved; marriage as a life-long partnership, with no sexual relations outside it; scrupulous honesty; avoidance of coveting, or longing to possess what belongs to others, including wealth and married partners.

Living by these, and similar principles, has always needed courage in a world which has other standards and principles.

Early churches were built on an east–west axis, but the sacred end could be the west, rather than the east (e.g. at Verulam Hills Field; and Silchester). At the prayer of consecration, the celebrant always faced east.

Sun worship still lingered in a half-pagan society; and Pope Leo the Great (440–61), preaching in St. Peter's, Rome, with its west altar, rebuked the congregation for bowing to the rising sun before entering the main eastern door. When the church was rebuilt, an eastern sanctuary was created so that sun-worship merged with reverence to Christ— originating the habit of bowing eastward at Jesus' name in the Creed.

The Roman basilica or aisled hall, with its apse or rounded end, influenced larger church plans, especially in towns.

In a narthex, or ante-chamber, candidates for baptism were instructed and heard the first part of the Eucharist before being dismissed. Separate baptistries were built close by, with steps descending into a shaped stone basin for complete or partial immersion.

As Christianity spread, parents brought children for baptism, leaving its completion until they were old enough for instruction to make responsible vows themselves. Meantime, as today, proxy vows were made by god-parents, acting as sureties for the child's instruction, and later making vows personally before the bishop, who would confirm them by anointing and laying on of hands.

Fonts, large enough to immerse infants, were introduced to the narthex or close to the entrance. Ancient churches were usually near springs of 'living water', the words font and fountain having the same derivation.

The body of the church, the nave (Latin, *navis*, a ship), symbolised the vessel of salvation carrying Christians across life's stormy seas. (This imagery, inspired by Noah's ark saving human beings and animals from the flood, influenced the baptism service.) Usually the congregation stood, wall-benches being provided for the aged and infirm.

In the apse, reached by steps beneath a triumphal arch, a semi-circular bench for clergy had a central seat for the bishop.

In front stood the Lord's Table (Latin, *mensa Domini*) within four pillars supporting a canopy and rich hangings on all four sides. Before the consecration of bread and wine, these curtains were drawn aside and the bishop, or, in his absence, a presbyter (Greek, *presbyteros*, an elder) moved to the people's side.

Between the Lord's Table and the congregation lay a rectangular enclosure for assistant clergy and singers, open to the sanctuary, but defined to north and south by low screens. Outside each stood an ambo, or enclosed desk, approached by steps, for reading Scripture passages. The remaining side had a central opening from the nave.

Fifth- and sixth-century Anglo-Saxon invaders destroyed churches of early types; but details can be recovered from excavations, contemporary writings and comparison with continental examples.

Rudston (All Saints), *North Humberside: six miles due west of Bridlington, with its early Norman west tower, shares a low mound with the tallest monolith in England, twenty-five feet high and perhaps as much below ground. Just west, rises a spring of fresh water. Neolithic people brought the stone from near Scarborough c. 3000–2000 B.C. for religious purposes. The church often re-used such sites, as new Christians, still half-pagan, could reverence Christ in a familiar place. Nearby was a magnificent Roman villa and the Roman road to York.*
The late W. Dodds

THE CHURCH BEFORE 597

About 357, Ninian began evangelistic work in Cumbria and southern Scotland. From the monastery he founded at Whithorn in Galloway, monks took the Gospel both along Hadrian's Wall and further north.

At this period a boy named Patrick, son of Calpornus, a deacon, and grandson of a priest, was captured on the west coast and sold into slavery in Ireland. He escaped, trained for the ministry, and in *c.* 432 was consecrated bishop to return to Ireland and died about 461. He founded many Celtic monasteries, within whose banked enclosures were contained round 'beehive-shaped' huts for individual monks, a rectangular stone church and other communal buildings.

After the Roman armies left mainland Britain, the people considered themselves a Christian society, although falling short in practice; but Angles, Saxons and Jutes soon invaded the eastern and southern coasts bringing militant Teutonic paganism and destroying churches wherever they conquered and settled.

Christianity was driven to the far north, the south-west, and Wales, where, in remote places, headlands and islands, monastic communities kept faith alive and nurtured saints like the abbot-bishop David (*c.* 520–88).

In his time was born, in 521, the royal Columba, who attended school in one of Patrick's monasteries. He left Ireland in 563 with twelve companions, landing on Iona, an island off the west coast of Scotland. There he founded a Celtic-type monastery from which he and his followers made missionary journeys as far north as the Orkneys. He died on Iona on 9th June 597.

THE ROMAN MISSION OF ST. AUGUSTINE

Eight days before St. Columba's death in 597, St. Augustine and his monks landed in Kent, whose king, Ethelbert, received them warmly, and many were baptised. They found his Christian wife, Bertha, using St. Martin's, Canterbury, probably a survival from Roman times.

Unfortunately, the British (Celtic) church had not evangelised the Anglo-Saxon invaders. St. Augustine hoped to remedy this. About 601, he was joined by an Italian monk, Paulinus, who, after working in the south, was consecrated bishop in 625 to accompany Princess Ethelburga of Kent to her marriage with Edwin, King of Northumbria. Paulinus preached to the king's court, and Edwin was baptised at York on Easter Eve, 627. The ensuing Northumbrian mission seemed a spectacular success, but in 633, Edwin was killed in battle at Heavenfield, near Hexham, by the British Cadwallon and Paulinus fled south. His work—perhaps superficial—collapsed. One man,

James the Deacon, remained near Catterick to support faithful Christians.

Other contemporaries of Augustine's mission in London, East Anglia, and Wessex, made little permanent impression.

Bewcastle (St. Cuthbert), *Cumbria: the cross (the head is lost) erected in 670 by Ecgfrith, King of Northumbria, in memory of the sub-king Alcfrith, son of Oswy. It stands outside the west end of the twelfth-century church (reconstructed 1792). West face: top—John the Baptist bears the Lamb of God (representing Christ); below—Christ triumphant over evil, symbolised by the lion and adder under his feet; next—the runic memorial inscription; bottom—a falconer, perhaps Alcfrith, hawk on wrist, gentling rod in right hand, and perch below. South and north faces: panels of knot-work and vine-scroll, with a sundial on the south side. East face: a full-length panel with squirrels, birds and other creatures among the foliage and fruit of a vine-scroll (Jesus' discourse in John 15: 1–7, etc.). Church and castle lie within the site of Banna, a Roman fort built c. A.D. 120 as a north-western outpost of Hadrian's Wall.* Jean Anderson

Holy Island (Lindisfarne) *is cut off from mainland Northumberland by the tide twice a day, but is accessible over a causeway at low water. Given by Oswald, King and Saint, to Bishop Aidan to found a monastery, it lies within sight of the old royal fortress of Bamburgh.* *Margot Johnson*

THE IRISH MISSION FROM IONA

King Edwin's nephew, Oswald, was sent to Iona in 617 on his father's death and educated by the monks. Now a man, he drove out the heathen invaders, united the two Northumbrian kingdoms and began to reign from Bamburgh in 635.

Wishing to evangelise his people, he sent at once to Iona for a bishop. When St. Aidan arrived, he gave him Lindisfarne (Holy Island) to found a monastery like Iona. From its school, missionaries spread the faith widely. Cedd founded churches and monasteries in Essex and north Yorkshire; his brother Chad went to York and later to Mercia; and, later, Wilfred preached as far south as Selsey.

Missionaries from the Celtic church (except Wilfred, who visited Rome and took Benedictine monasticism to Hexham and Ripon) had different traditions from the Roman mission, including another way to calculate the date of Easter. Oswy, King of Northumbria, called a Synod at Whitby under the Abbess Hilda in 664, when the differences were settled in favour of Roman customs.

In a transitional period, St. Cuthbert, abbot of Lindisfarne from 664 and bishop 684–6, accepted the Synod's decision, but remained true to Celtic ideals of piety and humility. He died a hermit in 687.

THE SEVENTH-CENTURY CHURCH

During St. Cuthbert's lifetime, many died of plague and church organisation suffered. Leaders were few and when Theodore of Tarsus, then aged sixty-six, was sent to become Archbishop of Canterbury, the see had been vacant five years. He arrived there in 669 with two other monks: Hadrian, a learned North African; and Benedict Biscop, of Northumbrian stock. Finding only three bishops in England, he moved Chad from York to Lichfield; gave Wilfred, then Bishop of Ripon, charge of all Northumbria; and consecrated three new bishops for the south. At his

death in 690, schools at Canterbury, York, Hexham and Ripon provided a broad education for future clergy; while the monasteries taught intending monks. Benedict Biscop became abbot of St. Augustine's monastery, Canterbury, before moving north to found a Benedictine house at Monkwearmouth in 674 and its twin at Jarrow in 685.

He imported continental craftsmen to build in stone, make coloured window-glass, and create wall-paintings of Biblical scenes—visual aids for an illiterate people; and brought back many manuscripts

Monkwearmouth (St. Peter), *Tyne and Wear: founded as a monastery by Benedict Biscop in 674 on land granted by Ecgfrith, King of Northumbria. The west wall had originally a doorway at its south end (suggesting a west altar), blocked when a little later a central door and porch were added, the latter the burial place of Eosterwine (d. 685) the first abbot appointed by Biscop. The porch has arched openings, decorated with intertwined creatures; above are faint traces of a large figure sculptured in relief. The fourth stage and belfry of the tower are late pre-Conquest. The church had an eastern apse and north and south porticus, but was rebuilt in the fourteenth century. The north aisle was added in 1874. The adjacent monastic site has been excavated extensively.* G. Dresser

from his numerous travels abroad to form a remarkable library. Some books survive today.

Bede, born in Northumbria in 673, entered Biscop's monastery when seven years old, survived the plague at twelve (the only other survivor was the abbot) and achieved international fame as a scholar, owing much to the fine library. He introduced into this country our present manner of dating B.C. and A.D. and wrote about forty books. His *History of the English church and people* remains the most important source for his own and earlier times. For his accuracy and carefully checked use of the material he assembled, he has been called 'the father of English historians'. He died at Jarrow in 735.

Bede mentions much new monastic and church building, as well as Christian adaptation of pagan religious sites, emphasising also the importance of having a resident priest in every local community.

Larger churches or minsters (monastic churches) usually had an apse, as in the older basilicas. Side chambers or *porticus* were attached to the north and south walls, each entered by its own door from the nave, and later used for important burials. Above them, an upper floor could be inserted. Such churches had an outside covering of hard plaster, fresco-painted walls inside, and towers and altars at both east and west ends. Where there was a central west door, the altar was in a gallery above (e.g. Deerhurst, Gloucestershire). Windows were high and small, and roofs lofty.

Smaller churches were tall and and narrow. Their unglazed windows, closed by shutters, were high enough to lessen the congregation's discomfort.

Escomb Church, *County Durham (no known early dedication): the unaltered north side, typical of early Saxon work. The church is built of ashlars from the nearby Binchester Roman fort. A vanished north porticus, entered through the blocked doorway, overlapped nave and chancel. The high, small windows, deeply splayed inside, were shuttered, but unglazed. The east window, two twelfth-century lancets on the south side, and the south porch are the only alterations. A former west annexe perhaps housed the priest.* G. Dresser

FESTIVALS, FASTS AND SACRAMENTS

Christians, like Jews, have always been convinced that their religion is no mere matter of rites and ceremonies, but involves all aspects of life.

Both believe that certain acts are God-given and signs of his grace. From Jewish baptism, initiating Gentile converts to the synagogue, Christian baptism developed as admission to the church. Both expect repentance—turning from sin. The bread and wine of the Passover meal acquired new meaning in Christ's words and acts at the Last Supper.

In New Testament times, Christians met already each Sunday, known as the 'Lord's Day' because of the Resurrection. Soon Easter, celebrated at Passover (always the fourteenth day of the month Nisan) was developed and was naturally fixed on the Sunday following, as Sundays were already festivals of the Resurrection.

The Jewish Pentecost, when the first Christians received the Holy Spirit in 'tongues of fire', became next in importance in the Christian calendar.

The nativity (Christmas) was added at the winter solstice, the 'birthday' of the Roman invincible sun-god, after Constantine became a Christian in the fourth century, though the belief that Jesus was born in winter can be traced back to the beginning of the third century; Ascension Day, forty days after Easter, was already known at that period.

Jews fasted on Mondays and Thursdays; and Christians, by the end of the first century, on Wednesdays and Fridays. Fast days were called 'stations', days of 'military watch duty' against sin; and the special forty-day fast before Easter—Lent —was kept in the fourth century.

A description of the Eucharist in about 150 shows its celebration had a commonly accepted framework, but no set form of words. Soon, forms at first provided as patterns became accepted use, and parts survive today. Fourth-century writings reveal increasingly elaborate ceremonial and a great reverence for the Lord's Table.

Services were not uniform in the Western church. The Roman rite, used in Rome and some, but not all, parts of Italy by 400, came to Britain with St. Augustine.

By the late eighth century, the varied forms in Britain had been reduced to two: the Roman and the Gallican (used by the Irish) which may have had its origins in Ephesus. Both forms were used in Northumbria.

Alcuin of York (d. 796) was commissioned to enlarge the austere Roman rite. His work was so successful, it replaced gradually the original form throughout the Western church.

THE DAILY SERVICES

The daily offices (Latin *officium*, divine service) were drawn from the Bible, mostly the Psalter. They grew out of the practice, known from *c.* 200, of daily house prayers and family Bible reading on rising, when the evening lamp was lit, at bedtime, and at midnight. When at home, Christians prayed also at the third, sixth and ninth hours (our 9 a.m., noon and 3 p.m.), the hours associated with Christ's Passion (Latin *patior*, suffer). As in synagogue services, dignified language was preferred to everyday speech; and by 400, on some weekdays clergy led morning and evening prayers for large congregations.

In monasteries, daily prayers developed to include reading the whole Psalter weekly, with Psalm 119, the longest, at Terce, Sext and None, the Offices of the third, sixth and ninth hours.

St. Benedict of Nursia founded Benedictine monasticism in about 529. In his Rule he added Prime and Compline (Latin *completorium*) to begin and end each day. The Office began: 'O God make speed to save me. O Lord make haste to help me', followed by the *Gloria* ('Glory be to the Father, and to the Son, and to the Holy Ghost. As it was in the beginning, is now, and ever shall be, world without

end. Amen'.). Benedict included in the offices the hymns of St. Ambrose (bishop of Milan 373–97) and, for Saturday evenings, the ancient *Te Deum* ('We praise thee O God, we acknowledge thee to be the Lord . . .').

At Lauds, the dawn Office, he added the *Benedictus*, the prophetic hymn of Zacharias after the birth of his son, John the Baptist, who heralded Jesus' ministry: 'Blessed be the Lord God of Israel; for he hath visited and redeemed his people . . .' (Luke 1: 68–79). Benedict included in Lauds also the *Benedicite*, 'O all ye works of the Lord, bless ye the Lord . . .', the song of the Three Holy Children (Daniel and his companions) in the burning fiery furnace (Apocrypha). This had been used widely in the Greek church before 400.

St. Augustine and his monks brought developed daily offices to Britain in 597.

Benedict's Compline did not include the *Nunc Dimittis*, 'Lord, now lettest thou thy servant depart in peace, according to thy word: for mine eyes have seen thy salvation . . .', which is the Song of Simeon (Luke 2: 29–32) when the infant Jesus was brought to the Jerusalem Temple; but the Greek church used it at evening prayers by the late fourth century. Later, it became part of the Roman rite.

The *Magnificat*, the hymn of Mary after the Angel announced her conception of Jesus (Luke 1: 46–55), 'My soul doth magnify the Lord . . .', was used by the early sixth century in Arles (to which Roman Britain had been attached). It was known in Ireland in the seventh century and probably St. Columba took it to Iona. St. Aidan carried the Irish Offices to Northumbria. From there they spread with the Lindisfarne missions.

THE LATER PRE-CONQUEST CHURCH

From the late eighth century onwards, waves of Danish and Viking invaders raided the coastal monasteries, almost extinguishing the Church in the north and east, and bringing back paganism.

However, missionary work revived as the invaders became settlers. Surviving stone buildings were restored and adapted; large churches were reduced by demolishing porticus and blocking their doors, leaving the special burials in the open air.

New, larger churches and cathedrals were copies from those of Carolingian Gaul (France). These, unlike later churches, had transepts or wings at both ends as well as altars. If there was a west door, a gallery over it held another altar. Towers at both ends of the nave were usual; and turrets contained spiral stairs to upper floors. Outside, the plastered walls were decorated with pilasters (decorative stone strips).

Small parish churches tended to be of wood. One survives from the tenth century at Greenstead, Essex and is built from split oak logs.

In the tenth century the daily offices were known as 'uht-song, prime-song, undern-song, mid-day-song, noon-song, evensong, and night-song'. There were seven in remembrance of the Psalmist's, 'Seven times a day will I praise thee'. The laity were encouraged to use them; and urged to attend evensong and

Brixworth (All Saints), *Northamptonshire: founded in the seventh century as the result of the Lindisfarne mission, it was later sacked by the Danes. Its ten nave porticus or side-chambers are lost. Their arches of Roman tiles are blocked and Norman windows and doors inserted. The west doorway connected formerly with a narthex of three parts, partly under the tower. Beyond the presbytery (choir) the apse had a ring crypt, probably connected with relics displayed below the altar. A reliquary found in 1821, walled up in the thirteenth-century south chantry chapel, contains a larynx bone (of St. Boniface?).* K. Yates

night-song (Nocturns) on Saturdays in preparation for the Sunday Eucharist. Attendance at High Mass was preferred to the early Low Mass, as the latter might encourage misuse of free hours on Sunday.

The Sabbath (Hebrew, *shabat*, ceasing) was kept free from work from Saturday afternoon until Monday morning; for Sunday, the first day of the week, on which Christ rose from the dead, had long replaced the Jewish Saturday Sabbath.

At the Eucharist, wine was consecrated in a large chalice (Latin, *calyx*, cup) with two handles for carrying it to the people who knelt at the foot of the sanctuary steps. Often, lay people received wine not directly from the chalice (as today), but through a long, narrow tube or pipe of silver or ivory, attached by a chain and sometimes secured by a pivot to the lower inside part of the vessel. Such 'reeds' of precious materials were among the treasures distributed to the greater churches and monasteries by William Rufus, in accordance with the wishes of his father, William I. They were in general use until the chalice was forbidden to the people by the thirteenth century.

The whole country was divided into parishes. Their boundaries usually coincided with those of estates, whose lord built the church. He appointed its priest, often a local man, who farmed his strips in the common fields like his parishioners. They gave him, originally voluntarily, tithes (tenths) of their arable and animal crops and some other dues to uphold his office and responsibilities, which included maintaining the fabric of the church's chancel. He was expected to teach their children, and also kept the bull and boar to service their animals. He had a two-fold allegiance: to the lord, and to his bishop, who instituted him, and could not be removed except for grave misconduct.

Deerhurst (Odda's Chapel), *Gloucestershire: built (perhaps re-using an older building) by Earl Odda, friend of Edward the Confessor, in memory of his brother Aelfric, and dedicated to the Holy Trinity on 12 April 1056. Until 1539 it was part of Abbot's Court, a lodge of the Abbot of Westminster, and later was absorbed into a Tudor farmhouse. Its true nature was revealed in 1885. It stands opposite the west end of Deerhurst Church, formerly the Priory Church and dating from the seventh century.* Margot Johnson

THE NORMAN CONQUEST AND LATER

William the Conqueror saw himself as a church reformer and introduced clergy from Normandy. Many Saxon churches were either demolished and rebuilt or modified to new styles. New buildings were plain, rectangular if small (e.g. Heath, Shropshire), or with eastern apses if larger, and orientated, perhaps by the rising sun on the day they were planned on the ground. Towers were rare; but a single bell in a bell-cote called to worship, or announced the consecration of bread and wine..

North or south doors generally formed the main entrances. Just within stood the font, a stone basin on a pedestal. Infant baptism was now universal.

Walls were coated outside with hard plaster; and inside plasterwork was brilliant with paintings in gold, black, white, red, ochre and blue, illustrating Bible stories, saints' lives, or legends intended to edify.

At the east end, the small paved chancel (Latin, *cancelli*, cross-bars, lattice) was separated from the nave by a parclose screen of iron-work, carved wood, or stone, partly closing the narrow, and often low, chancel arch. This fostered a sense of mystery in the sacred area beyond.

The wooden altar, commonly called 'Christ's Board', stood at the east end. In 1076, the Council of Winchester under Archbishop Lanfranc ordered altars to be of stone, but was not always obeyed. These were squarish and inscribed with crosses, one in each corner and one in the centre, symbolizing the Five Wounds inflicted on Christ at the Crucifixion.

The chalice and paten (Latin, *patena*, plate for eucharistic bread) were kept in a locked aumbry or wall-cupboard north of the altar. In the east wall a similar aumbry might contain relics. Today, many

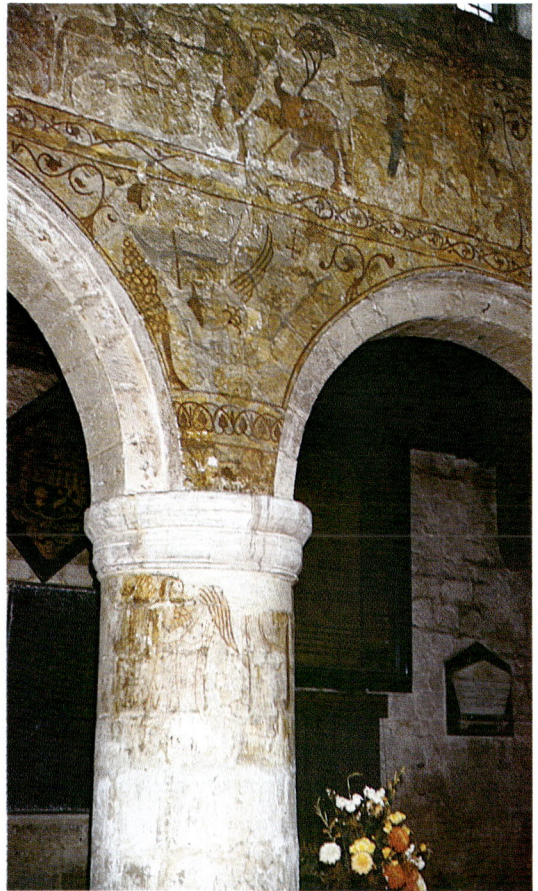

Claverley (All Saints), *Shropshire: the pre-Conquest north wall, pierced by a late eleventh-century arcade. The long frieze of c. 1200 suggests a painter acquainted with the Bayeux tapestry. It illustrates a poem of Prudentius (c. A.D. 348–410), called* Psychomachia, *part of a popular medieval book, describing in allegory the Christian struggle against paganism. Pairs of knights on horseback represent the seven Christian virtues fighting the seven pagan vices. Under the nave lie remains of a substantial Roman building on which the first Saxon church was built.*   Margot Johnson

early aumbries lack doors or hide behind later panelling. An ornamental niche in the south wall held the piscina, a stone basin and drain to carry away water used for washing altar vessels and the priest's hands after Mass, as directed *c.* 850 by Pope Leo IV. After Pope Innocent, in the thirteenth century, required priests to wash their hands also before Mass, a second, simpler piscina appeared beside a more elaborate eastern one reserved for altar vessels. When, in the fourteenth century, it became customary for priests to drink the ablutions—water which had rinsed the paten and chalice—a single piscina again became usual. Sometimes a credence shelf was made above the basin for the wafer box and cruets of wine and water; and grooves for a wooden shelf remain.

Occasionally, especially in monastic churches, a floor drain was made for pouring away a little water and wine before use, in case the surface had attracted dust.

Near the piscina were the sedilia, stone (or sometimes wood) canopied seats for the priest, deacon and sub-deacon at High Mass, the celebrant occupying the high eastern seat of a set of two, three or even four in large churches (e.g. Stratford-on-Avon). Later sedilia were at one level when priests performed the duties of all three officiants.

The congregation in the nave brought stools, stood, or walked about, while the aged or infirm might have wall benches ('the weakest go to the wall'). The nave floor, of beaten earth in smaller churches, was strewn with rushes, renewed periodically. Earth piled in one corner was common as burials took place within the building.

Services were in Latin, the language of the educated, and little understood by lay people, few of whom could read. A few clergy could preach, but many could not. Inattention was usual, hence the Sanctus Bell, normally rung from a bell-cote to secure silence for the consecration of the bread and wine.

From the thirteenth century, lay people were refused the chalice and received communion rarely, eventually only at Easter and then only in bread. As the priest alone consumed wine, chalices became very small.

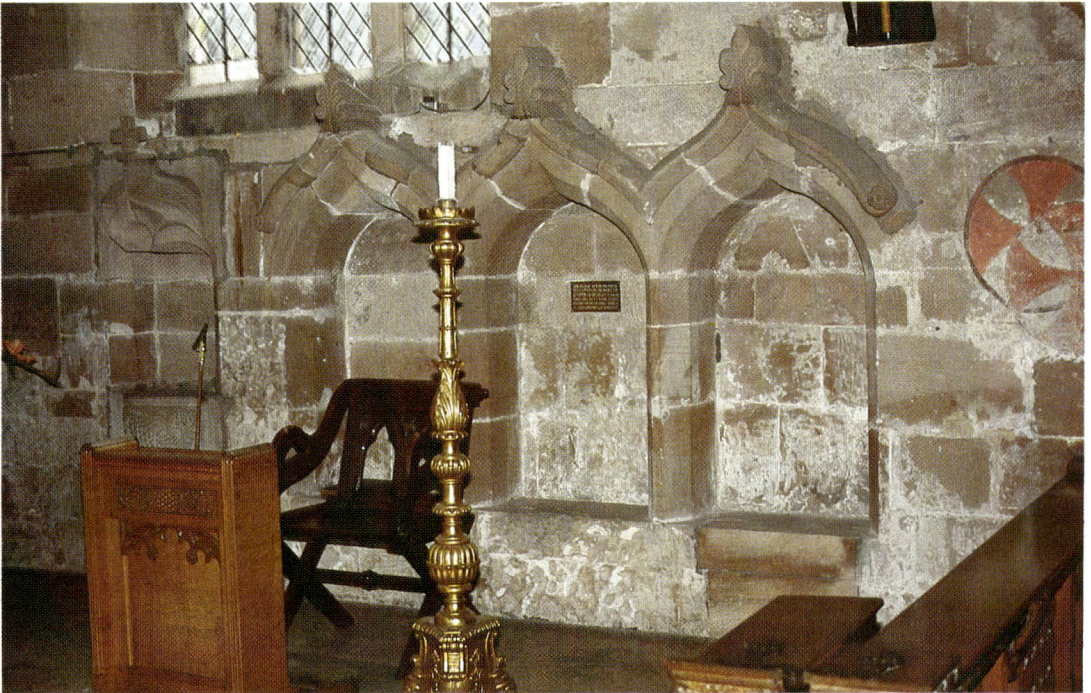

Claverley (All Saints), *Shropshire: the triple sedilia with the piscina, left, and two consecration crosses, right. The church has also an early Saxon font; another of the eleventh century; a porch chamber; the rood loft door above a fine Jacobean pulpit; remains of the Doom painting over the chancel arch; two chapels; fine sixteenth-century monuments; and much else of interest.*   Margot Johnson

THE TWELFTH TO FIFTEENTH CENTURIES

Churches began to alter greatly in appearance. West towers became fashionable and, as glazing grew less expensive, wider and lower windows with wood or stone mullions were inserted. The stone carvers' skills produced fine tracery. Square-ended chancels with large east windows often replaced eastern apses. The stone altar, placed against the east wall, had curtains on three sides (dorsals and riddels) or a carved rear screen (reredos).

By *c.* 1300, English churches used some form of the Roman rite, with local variations, from two groups of service books: those for Divine Service (now eight Daily Offices); and those for the Sacraments, and other Offices. The first group contained the Psalter (with Canticles—Biblical hymns such as the *Magnificat*); the Antiphonary (anthems); the Responsionary (responds to Lessons); the Bible (Lessons); the Homiliary (sermons); the Hymnary (hymns); and some other books. The second group included the Sacramentary (prayers at the Eucharist and other services); the Gradual (parts of the Eucharist sung by the choir); the Lectionary (lessons and epistles at the Eucharist); and the Gospel Book (gospels). Another book, the Ordo, contained rules for singing the services in both groups.

All services, readings, anthems and hymns were in Latin.

Daily offices, begun to express love of Christ, became an end in themselves. Their recital became a task intended to secure God's favour after death.

Money might be given to a monastery, or other large church, for prayers to be said for the departed; but towards the end of the twelfth century, wealthy families began to endow chantries, providing the stipend for a priest to say Mass and the Office for the Dead daily, and in perpetuity, for the soul of the founder, his family and descendants, at first at existing altars.

Soon, however, special chapels were added to parish churches. Part of the original nave wall was rebuilt some feet further out and replaced by a pillared arcade, forming a separately roofed aisle. This held chantry chapels, each with its altar and tombs of the founder and his family, often with richly carved and coloured recumbent effigies. Wood or stone screens of fine craftsmanship separated each chapel from the church itself.

Occasionally chantries were in separate buildings, such as the former bridge chapels at Durham.

Pittington (St. Laurence), *County Durham: a twelfth-century arcade pierces the pre-Conquest north wall, creating an aisle for chantry chapels. The original high windows now look into the aisle, their wide splays embellished with important twelfth-century paintings of scenes from the life of St. Cuthbert. The later clerestory increases light in the nave.* G. Dresser

In towns, groups of inhabitants founded guilds to provide chantries for those who could not afford to act privately.

So that chantry priests could say Daily Offices with the incumbent (rector or vicar), and help to lead Sunday services, chancels were lengthened and fitted with stalls (centre-facing seats and desks). The incumbent's stall was next to the screen.

By the late fourteenth century, most churches had long chancels and chantry chapels. Chancel stalls became elaborate, fronted with wainscot and often canopied above against draughts. In larger churches their seats tipped up to reveal elaborately carved ledges beneath—misericords—on which chaplains might rest in a standing position during long psalms.

As a chantry priest's duties were light, he could undertake other tasks and often taught local children. In some places (e.g. Tong, Staffordshire) chaplains formed an independent body to serve many chantries in a parish church. Another arrangement was a separate foundation, like St. George's, Windsor. Some chantry foundations had educational aims, or a school attached, as at Eton.

From the fifteenth century, Easter Sepulchres of wood, or carved stone set in the sanctuary's north wall, also became customary. Wood examples (e.g. at Durham Cathedral and St. Edmund's Salisbury) have vanished; but fine stone ones survive at Patrington (North Humberside), and Hawton (Nottinghamshire). The latter was combined with the founder's tomb and north chantry chapel. Below its shelf lie sculptured sleeping Roman guards; above are angels.

On Good Friday evening the altar cross, wrapped in a napkin, was placed on the shelf to represent Christ's burial. Early on Easter Day it was replaced on the altar. Three assistant clergy approached the Sepulchre, representing the women of the Gospels seeking to complete the burial customs. Another cleric, seated near the Sepulchre as the Angel, answered their questions saying, 'He is not here, he is risen!'. These rituals developed into full dramas performed in church until, becoming distractions from worship, they moved into the streets as miracle plays.

Complementing long chancels were high, wide chancel arches, closed by elaborately carved and

Tewkesbury Abbey, *Gloucestershire: the Beauchamp chapel (one of several ornate chantry chapels), erected by Isabella Despenser, heiress of the manor of Tewkesbury, over the tomb of her first husband, Richard Beauchamp. Begun in 1422, it took sixteen years to build, being finished the year before her death. The chapel has two storeys: the lower one is fan-vaulted, and three niches against the west wall probably once framed the kneeling figures of Isabella and her two Beauchamp husbands, the Earls of Worcester and Warwick. The upper storey has mini-lièrne vaulting. It has no stair and its purpose is unknown. This church, 'deemed to be superfluous' at the Dissolution in 1539, was bought for £453 (the valuation of the roof lead and bells) by the townspeople, who had used the nave as their parish church from its foundation.*
Roger Dauncey

Sulgrave (St. James the Less), *Northamptonshire: the little door below the perpendicular window once helped to ventilate an enclosed chancel. Similar apertures elsewhere have usually been converted into 'low-side windows'. The south aisle of this fourteenth-century church contains, at its east end, the tomb of Lawrence Washington, his wife Amee, and his son Robert. Lawrence, builder of Sulgrave Manor House, and ancestor of George Washington, first president of the United States of America, bought from Henry VIII in 1539, for £324 14s. 10d., the lands he held in Sulgrave and elsewhere as tenant of St. Andrew's Priory, Northampton.*
Canon S. Brown

painted screens supporting rood lofts or galleries reached by stairs.

The rood, or cross, bearing the figure of Christ crucified, stood centrally, with statues of the Virgin Mary and St. John on either side—the only two people to remain beside the dying Jesus. Torches were kept burning before them.

In larger churches, the rood loft contained a small organ and, especially at festivals, singers and musicians.

Behind the rood, the Doom or Last Judgment was painted imaginatively, either on a wood panel filling the arch, or on the wall above, reminding worshippers that only Christ's sacrifice on the cross stood between them and a disagreeable fate.

The chancel, entered by the laity only on special occasions such as Easter, to receive Holy Communion (now only annually), represented a foretaste of Heaven, The altar had rich coverings and either dorsals and riddels (back and side hangings) or an elaborately carved reredos. Above, as in Saxon times, hung a 'corona' or wide circle of many lamps.

Within the screen, near the incumbent's stall, might be a low shuttered opening to ventilate the chancel, whose confined atmosphere grew heavy with the fumes of many torches, lights and the scent of incense.

Before the chancel screen at one side stood the pulpit, richly carved in wood or stone. The separate lectern or reading desk, opposite, often represented an eagle, holding the book on wings outstretched as though for heavenward flight. One is recorded at Salisbury in 1214; another appears in the Luttrell Psalter, a manuscript of *c.* 1300. Some eagles had beaks open to receive offerings which could be removed, as at Southwell, by a 'door' under the tail. Eagles were chosen to symbolise St. John, whose Gospel dwells on Jesus' discourses. An alternative lectern bird was the 'pelican in her piety', so-called from the legend that she tears her breast to feed her young, representing the Christian's feeding on Eucharistic bread and wine.

Middleham (Hampshire) has an oak pelican; and a brass example of *c.* 1375 at Norwich Cathedral was 'improved' in 1845 by adding figures of bishop, priest and deacon round the shaft! Additionally, some chancels had a small, two-sided lectern; or a built-in stone lectern near the altar for reading the Gospel at Mass. At Buckley (Oxfordshire) a similar lectern near the font probably held the Manual containing the baptism service.

Above the colourful walls, pillars and woodwork, later medieval roofs were enriched usually with painted panels; blue sprinkled with stars; coats of arms; royal heads and other devices; and beams had supporting carved heads or coloured figures. Angels in flowing robes and carrying trumpets were popular in larger churches.

BAPTISM, MARRIAGE, PENANCE, UNCTION AND BURIAL

These had acquired a new character before the Reformation.

Baptism began outside the church door, in the porch. The infant, brought by the father and godparents on the day of birth, underwent long and complicated ceremonies in addition: exorcism of evil spirits; 'unction' with spittle; anointing with oil; and wrapping in the white chrisom cloth which the mother returned when she came to be churched (the thankgiving for safe delivery). At the font itself, the baby was immersed. (The priest placed one hand over the nose and mouth to prevent drowning.) Confirmation followed when the child could walk and usually before three years old, ignoring the need for responsible vows; some bishops neglected confirmation altogether.

Marriage vows were made, in English during the Latin service, outside in the church porch where the whole community could witness the proceedings. Chaucer wrote of the Wyf of Bath: 'husbands at churchë door she haddë five'—she had been married five times! Afterwards, the wedding party went inside to the altar steps for Nuptial Mass. Later, the priest visited the couple in bed and sprinkled them with holy water.

Auricular confession, made compulsory c. 1215, with detailed enquiries into faith and morals, was conducted usually at the chancel entrance and preceded the annual communion at Easter.

The Visitation of the Sick was encouraged; but Unction, originally a healing sacrament of anointing, had become preparation for death.

At a rich person's funeral the coffin was placed in a hearse, a wrought-iron frame holding lighted candles; but the majority were wrapped in a cere-cloth—a waxed shroud—and carried in an open coffin on the parish bier to an uncoffined burial.

All who could afford it were interred in 'lair-stalls' in the church, so that usually there was a pile of earth in one corner. The nave floor became paved largely with 'lair-stones', flat slabs often inscribed with a cross, the style varying with the period of burial, and symbols showing the occupation or status of

Claverley (All Saints), *Shropshire: the fine eleventh-century font replaced an early Saxon 'tub' font, still in the church, and may relate to the probable rebuilding by Leofric, Earl of Mercia (d. 1057), husband of the famous Lady Godiva. The door in the background leads to the porch chamber.* Margot Johnson

Brampton Abbotts (St. Michael and All Angels), *Herefordshire: built about 1100. Its fourteenth-century porch, restored but retaining all the ancient woodwork, protects a south doorway with scalloped capitals and plain tympanum. Near the fourteenth-century chancel arch are traces of the stair once leading to the rood-loft and higher. In the chancel is the head of a pillar piscina. The timber bell-turret, of 1686 or earlier, has an impressive substructure inside the church.* N. J. Dale

the deceased: shears—a cloth worker; a horn—a huntsman; a sword—a knight or gentlemen; scissors—a woman; a chalice—a priest (a chancel burial); and so on. Only a few bore names.

On important occasions, and especially at the bishop's or archdeacon's Visitation, juniper was scattered on the rush-strewn floor to sweeten the air. It could become unpleasant with the smell of decay from many burials near the surface. Incense was thought also to purify.

General lighting could be provided by chandeliers, some elaborate, where a private benefactor could afford the expense. A late fourteenth-century example of latten (an amalgam of brass) in the Temple church, Bristol, has two tiers of branches, the lower one of eight, the upper of four, with a crowned Virgin and Child above, St. George and the dragon below, and a grotesque head and ring for drawing down to clean or light. Simpler methods were to mount torches in a pricket—spikes in an oblong iron frame fastened at right angles to a wall; or by cressets, sets of bowls, four to five inches in diameter,

hollowed out of limestone. These held fat in which wicks were floated (e.g. at Weston, Yorkshire).

Nave benches, sometimes backless, were introduced before 1400 and by 1500 were common. Men sat on one side of the church; women on the other. In the south-west, bench ends were generally square; East Anglia favoured tall poppy-heads. This name, used from the fourteenth century, comes from the French *poupée*, a doll, puppet, or figure-head. Poppy-heads developed into saints, human heads, animals and fleur-de-lis.

Overleaf (pages 16 to 17): **How the Prayer Book was made.** *Reproduced from* Your Prayer Book *(1949), by kind permission of The Society for Promoting Christian Knowledge (SPCK).*

ANCIENT SOURCES .

A book by the reformer Martin Bucer, written while staying with Cranmer in 1549, also influenced the Ordinal.

THE FORM & MANNER OF MAKING AND CONSECRATING ARCHBISHOPS, BISHOPS, PRIESTS AND DEACONS 1549/50

Archbishop Hermann of Cologne had issued in 1536, an instruction called the ENCHEIRIDION, which influenced the Prayer Book.

THE ROMAN RITE

The Roman Pontificals used in England were the basis of the Ordinal.

The Roman Rite used by Luther was a chief source of his Litany, which influenced the English Litany.

Details from these two Roman Litanies appear in the English Litany.

YORK & BRIXEN

At the Pope's wish the Spanish Cardinal de Quiñones produced a revised Roman Breviary. Its second recension (1536) influenced both the Litany and other parts of the Prayer Book.

The CHIEF sources of the English Litany were the SALISBURY Processional, Portiforum and Manual.

The SALISBURY MISSAL supplied certain details to the Order of Communion, and, with the other SALISBURY BOOKS, supplied the main structure of the P.B. Services; the choice of Scripture for the Epistles and Gospels. Much of their matter was simply translated, adapted or paraphrased and used bodily.

The BYZANTINE Rite

The Liturgy of Constantinople had been printed in 1526 and 1528. It supplied a few details to the Litany and the Holy Communion, directly, and through the Order of Communion.

The MOZARABIC Rite

This was a non-Roman rite preserved in Spain. It was printed in 1500 and supplied some details to the Baptism Office.

LUTHER'S LITANY 1520

In 1543 Hermann, under Lutheran influence, caused the COLOGNE CHURCH ORDER to be made. It affected the P.B. of 1549 directly & through the Order of Communion, & the P.B. of 1552 as well.

The Chapter of Cologne answered the Church Order with the conservative ANTIDIDAGMA, 1544, also a source of the P.B.

Several other Lutheran CHURCH ORDERS published between 1540 & 1543 influenced the practice but not the doctrine of the P.B.

THE ENGLISH LITANY 1544

ENGLISH ORDER OF COMMUNION 1548

INCORPORATED IN

INCORPORATED IN

THE PRAYER BOOK OF 1549

SUPPLIED BY FAR THE GREATER PART OF THE MATTER

THE PSALTER 1549

The Psalter was sometimes

COVERDALE 1535

THE GREAT BIBLE 1539

MATTHEW'S BIBLE 1534

1531 Tyndale 1534

G
NT

OOK WAS MADE.

The English Litany was first sung in procession in St. Paul's Cathedral, on St. Luke's Day, Sunday October 18th 1545.

Hampton Court Conference January 1603/4

Between Sessions

...rdinal, revised, was incorporated in the P.B. of 1552, but was subsequently published separately until 1662.

The Prayer Book of 1549 was carefully criticized by BUCER in a book called the CENSURA Most of his objections were dealt with in 1552.

Another reformer, Peter Martyr, raised one objection which was met.

These three books were prevented from returning to the 1549 form by continual Puritan pressure, whose inspiration was not Luther but Calvin.

Three men, later bishops, were chiefly responsible for the revision of 1662. Their names were — Matthew Wren, Robert Sanderson, John Cosin.

At the Savoy Conference the puritan divines presented a number of 'Exceptions', some of which were met.

From 1553–1558, under Queen Mary, the Roman Rite as used in 1547 was restored.

From 1644–1660 the Prayer Book was banned by the Commonwealth.

THE PRAYER BOOK OF 1552

THE ELIZABETHAN PRAYER BOOK 1559

THE PRAYER BOOK of KING JAMES 1603/4

THE PRAYER BOOK OF 1662

A few but important changes

Corrections and some important additions

THE SCOTTISH PRAYER BOOK OF 1637

This supplied substantial additions

In 1550 Bishop Gardiner, in prison, defended his position by appealing to the P.B. of 1549. Some changes in the Holy Communion of 1552 seem to be due to a desire to remove the grounds of his case.

Disputation at the Savoy Conference March — June 1661.

...yer Book greatly influenced the Scottish Book, 1637, and also the language of the 1662 Book.

...he P.B., but was not incorporated in it until 1662.

RHEIMS New Testament (R.C.) 1582

THE BISHOPS' BIBLE 1568

THE AUTHORIZED VERSION 1611

Those who made the Authorized Version of the Bible, consulted all the earlier versions.

C.G.M.E.

ATTEMPTS AT IMPROVEMENT

Grave disquiet about the ignorance, superstition and merely formal religion of many nominally Christian people, began in the fourteenth century. Large numbers were pagan at heart and practised sub-Christian customs until long after the Reformation. In a materialistic age, the church failed to give a lead.

The Yorkshireman John Wyclif (1328–1384), an Oxford don most of his life, believed that all authority came direct from God; priests and lay people stood equal in God's sight; and that because of human unworthiness, none should hold office and exercise authority as of right.

After the Great Schism in 1378 with its two rival popes, the papacy was an easy target. Wyclif attacked negligent clergy, worldly bishops, and monasticism because it created separate groups within Christian society, besides having fallen from its original high ideals.

Concerned about the laity's ignorance and shocked by the popular doctrine of Transubstantiation (that Eucharistic bread and wine became substantially Christ's body and blood) he inspired the translation of the whole Bible into English by Nicholas of Hereford, John Purvey and others of his following.

Wycliffe's Bible was copied and circulated widely, especially by his followers, the Poor Preachers (later called Lollards) who travelled about preaching from Scripture. Because the movement excited unrest, an act was passed in 1401 enabling bishops to try them for heresy. Those who refused to recant were passed to the civil authority and publicly burnt. So began a long line of martyrs.

In theory, services offered a daily round of worship based on the whole Psalter recited in order weekly; the entire Bible read annually in daily portions; canticles and prayers; and special prayers, psalms and scripture readings associated with Baptism, the Eucharist, and certain other occasions since early times.

In practice, services were unsatisfactory. Clergy and monks had developed and complicated them, making correct performance difficult, besides adding to the church calendar numerous holy days with special observations. Also they were entirely in Latin, the language of learning and law, while normally people spoke English or its dialects.

By 1500, the contents of the earlier service books had been rearranged to form seven volumes: the Missal (everything for the Eucharist); the Portifery (everything for the Divine Service), so-called because a priest could carry one easily; the Manual (all offices used in a parish church); and the Processional (litanies and other material for processions); the Pie (supplementing these four books with rules for singing the services); the Pontifical (all rites performed by a bishop); and the Primer (the official book of private prayers).

Services varied in different dioceses. York and Hereford, for example, had their own 'Uses'. That of Salisbury, the Sarum Use, was the most famous and even spread to the continent.

English church music had reached high standards by this time and was famous also beyond our shores. Plainsong, brought to England by St. Augustine in 597, was encouraged later by St. Dunstan (909–88), scholar, artist, accomplished musician, and organ builder. After the Norman Conquest part-singing was introduced and liturgical music became more elaborate. Beginning in the thirteenth century, cathedrals and large parish churches had choirs of men and boys whose increasing skills gradually fostered polyphonic music (independent lines of melody performed in harmony) and encouraged new, non-liturgical works. Henry VI (1422–1461), himself a skilled musician, encouraged an English school of composition and John Dunstable (d.1453) became the leading composer in Europe.

For lay people who could read, *The Lay Folks' Mass Book*, written in French *c.* 1150, and translated into English *c.* 1300, described in rhyme the action of the Mass, with instructions when to stand, kneel, and sign with the cross, prayers to use during the service, and paraphrases of the Creed and the Lord's Prayer. For home use, Books of Hours or *Prymers* were popular, and contained the Hours of Our Lady; the seven Penitential Psalms; the fifteen Gradual Psalms; a litany; 'Matynes for dede men' (Office for the Dead); and 'A Commendation of all Christian Souls'.

In addition, the *Lay Folks' Catechism*, translated from Archbishop Thoresby's *Instructions* (1357), complaining of lay ignorance through the clergy's neglect of teaching, set out paraphrases of the Lord's Prayer and the Ten Commandments; Fourteen points of the faith, sacraments, vices and virtues; and Works of mercy.

These books, being manuscripts, were expensive and beyond the means of most people. After William Caxton, who learned printing in Cologne in 1471–2, founded his Westminster Press in 1476, printed books spread slowly and became less expensive.

The Bible, however, was interpreted allegorically rather than understood as history. In theory, hope of

Beverley (St. Mary), *Humberside: The Minstrels' Pillar, erected at the east end of the north arcade by the Guild of Minstrels or gleemen, founded by King Athelstan (927–39), which flourished after the Norman Conquest and into later medieval times. The five figures formerly held musical instruments. The six pillars of the arcade have corbels with angels bearing scrolls inscribed with the names of their donors. (Beverley Minster has a series of carvings of medieval musicians with instruments.)*   Margot Johnson

salvation continued to be based on Christ's sacrifice; but in practice people relied on the church's prayers, masses for the dead, and the intercessions of saints if their interest could be gained—often by making expensive pilgrimages. Lay people were taught to pray to the Virgin Mary through the *Ave Maria*, believing she would intercede for the most hardened sinners. The number of prayers offered was most important.

TOWARDS REFORMATION

New ideas came from the continent. The Renaissance began in Italy in the fourteenth century; and under its influence Desiderius Erasmus (1467–1536) took the New Learning to Rotterdam, and thence to England while visiting John Colet (1466–1519), Dean of St. Paul's. Erasmus settled first in Oxford, then in Cambridge, introducing study of the Greek New Testament in the universities.

Roger Bacon (*c.* 1214–92) had struggled vainly to establish a historical approach to Scripture; but with growing interest in analysing evidence, Dean Colet—scholar and reformer—abandoned accepted interpretation through allegory and mysticism to seek the writers' original meanings. Colet also founded St. Paul's school to give 153 poor boys a classical education.

In 1517, Martin Luther's declarations in Germany began a movement reaching Cambridge soon after 1520. Here, at the White Horse Tavern, a group met to read his works, discussing the doctrine of

Justification by Faith (Romans 1: 17), the sale of indulgences, and other controversial subjects. Members probably included Thomas Cranmer, Hugh Latimer, Nicholas Ridley, and Matthew Parker, all future bishops; but others—Thomas Bilney, John Frith and Robert Barnes—suffered death for their beliefs. Henry VIII (1509–47), poet, scholar, gifted musician and composer, could debate brilliantly with leading theologians, but disliked Luther's reformed teaching, treating as traitors any who disagreed with royal views. His attack on Luther's writings against medieval sacramental teaching earned him the Pope's title of 'Defender of the Faith', still used by English monarchs.

Ideas on church-state relationship were changing also. The established belief that the two were inseparable, the state's duty being to serve the church, gradually gave way to the view that each was independent, with the state predominating and the church providing the spiritual dimension for living.

THE BREACH WITH ROME

By 1527, Henry's wife Katharine of Aragon, his brother's widow, had borne him three sons and two daughters. All except Mary died in infancy, leaving no male heir.

Henry saw this as a judgement on marriage within the prohibited degrees (although after Papal

dispensation), and on the grounds of repentance for disobedience to God's laws ('. . . if a man shall take his brother's wife, it is an unclean thing . . . they shall be childless.' Leviticus 20: 21), sought annulment in order to marry Anne Boleyn. Cardinal Wolsey, chancellor and papal legate, applied to Rome

Minsterworth (St. Peter), *Gloucestershire: displays an altar frontal which is one of several embroideries pieced together from disused medieval priests' copes by Katharine of Aragon and her ladies, probably when she and Henry VIII stayed at nearby Sudeley Castle from July to September 1535. Part of the figure of Christ (c. 1382), missing from the cross on the Winchcombe embroidery (see p. 34) is incorporated here. In 1870 this small church, on the banks of the River Severn, replaced a medieval predecessor ravaged by floods. Above the nave capitals are sculptured allusions to the local fisheries, orchards, lush fruit and flowers.* Roger Dauncey

immediately; but Pope Clement VII, not daring to offend the Emperor Charles V, Katharine's nephew, who virtually held him prisoner, nor wishing to overthrow the dispensation of his predecessor, Pope Julius II, ordered his legates to proceed extremely slowly to gain time. Henry, exasperated, deprived Wolsey of his chancellorship for obeying a foreign power. He was arrested on a charge of high treason in 1530 and died travelling to London for trial.

Henry now followed Cranmer's suggestion of seeking academic opinions on his marriage from English and continental universities. The majority favoured annulment.

Papal authority was unpopular. Popes levied taxes; and presented Italian courtiers to English bishoprics and benefices; while appellants to Rome suffered long delays and often miscarriage of justice. It was not difficult, between 1532 and 1534, for Parliament to pass seven Acts which together severed the English church from Rome.

Archbishop Wareham died in 1532 and Cranmer was consecrated Archbishop of Canterbury on 30 March, 1533. After the second Act, disallowing appeals to Rome, Cranmer could pronounce Henry's marriage to Katharine null and void. By 1534, separation from Rome was complete and the Pope retaliated by excommunicating Henry.

Cranmer began to prepare English services, adapting for general use the eight choir offices, then often said in two groups, morning and evening.

Reforming bishops encouraged their clergy to preach, teach the Creed and Lord's Prayer, and read the Bible in English, besides denouncing false relics and superstitions. Unfortunately, undiscriminating zealots often destroyed beautiful objects.

THE DISSOLUTION OF THE MONASTERIES

To many people the Reformation in England is identified with the disappearance of monastic life; but reformation was a long and complicated process in which the dissolution of religious houses, although drastic in itself, played a relatively small part.

Monasticism had declined steadily since the thirteenth century, a few houses having already closed before the general survey of ecclesiastical property and revenue made for Henry VIII in 1534. Realising the wealth of the smaller monasteries, he ordered commissioners to report on them; and on scurrilous manufactured evidence, they were dissolved in 1536 and their property confiscated. Their inmates either transferred to larger houses or were pensioned. Except for a small rising in Lincolnshire in 1536 and the Pilgrimage of Grace in Yorkshire—signs of alarm at the King's high handedness rather than support for the monks—there was no opposition.

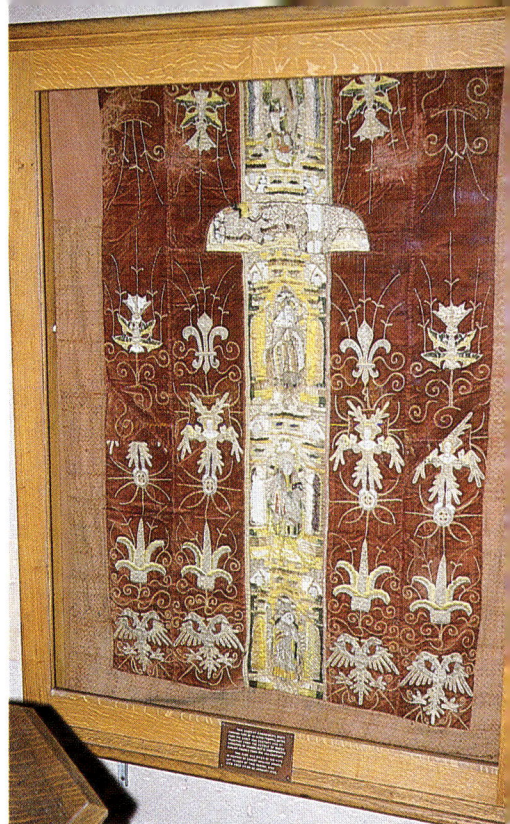

The friaries were closed in 1538; and in 1539, the larger monasteries were dissolved, their property yielding vast wealth to the crown. The abbots of Colchester, Glastonbury and Reading opposed closure and were hanged. Many religious received pensions; monks who were priests went to parishes; a few nuns ultimately married; and monastic servants either continued to work for the new landlords, or became unemployed. Some monastic churches became parish churches (e.g. Tewkesbury, Cartmel, Lanercost, etc.); monastic cathedrals continued with their abbot or prior and monks as the new secular dean and chapter; and six new dioceses were created at Bristol, Chester, Gloucester, Oxford, Peterborough, and Westminster, the monastic churches becoming their cathedrals.

Lay people in general, however, were unaffected. Religious changes were closer at hand.

BIBLE TRANSLATION

Wycliffe's English Bible was never widely available and William Tyndale, defying disapproval, worked on a new translation. In 1524, to escape death, he fled to Germany to continue its production, printing copies and smuggling them to England. His translation contained strongly Protestant notes; and he was betrayed, imprisoned, tried for heresy and executed in October 1536.

A year earlier, Miles Coverdale, a less able scholar, but with great literary ability, produced his translation and dedicated it to the King.

In 1537, Henry ordered Bibles in Latin and English to be placed in every church; but the problem of a suitable version arose. By 1538 the Great ('Cranmer's') Bible, based on both Tyndale's and Coverdale's work, was officially approved. People could now hear the Bible read in English, but English was not yet allowed in the services.

Little Sodbury (St. Adeline), *Avon: built on the village green in 1858, partly of material from the former church, whose remains stand near the Manor House. The stone pulpit commemorates five martyrs of the Reformation. The plain medieval wooden pulpit (right), lost for sixty years, was rescued from a barn at Bucklebury, near Reading, just before a 5 November bonfire c. 1968. William Tyndale preached from it in the former church in English after Mass, while tutor to the five grandchildren of John Walsh at the Manor House in 1522–3.*
*Nearby Horton Court (**Avon, National Trust**) was provided by Edward VI as a refuge for Edward Seymour, Duke of Somerset and Lord Protector, when Court enemies plotted against him. Somerset piloted the 1549 prayer book through parliament.*

The Rev. K. V. Ensor, Rector

ENGLISH SERVICES

The King disapproved of liturgical revision and English during services; but in 1542 the Sarum Use was ordered throughout England, so ending diversity among dioceses.

Many devout people blamed church services for ignorance and superstition among lay people. Continental changes began in the 1520s with Lutheran vernacular services and papal attempts to revise and shorten Latin rites. While in Germany in 1532, Cranmer attended services in German, afterwards keeping himself informed on both Lutheran and Catholic ideas and experiments.

Gradually, Henry relented about changes and in 1543 a chapter of the English Bible was ordered to be read at Matins and another at Evensong, so beginning our modern Lessons.

Cranmer was working already on English services, adapting for future general use the eight choir offices, then often said in two groups—morning and evening.

When, during war with France in 1544, Henry requested the customary prayers, he ordered Cranmer's English Litany for use in almost its present form. It is based on the Sarum *Processionale* which derives from a Greek liturgy brought to England *c.* 700.

Cartmel Fell (St. Antony), *Lancashire: this late pre-Reformation church has no structural chancel. The screen, formerly dividing chancel from nave, was re-used on the north side to surround the Cowmire Pew, later furnished with the school table. The medieval east window shows the 'Seven Sacraments'; on the wall at each side are the Lord's Prayer and the Creed; and the Decalogue (Ten Commandments) is handsomely displayed in an alcove at the north end of the sanctuary. The canopied Burblethwaite Pew and the three-tiered pulpit are seventeenth-century.* Basil Clarke

OUR ENGLISH CHURCH HERITAGE

from the beginning to 1662

by Margot Johnson, M.A., F.L.A.

Our English Church Heritage: from the beginning to 1662

by
Margot Johnson, M.A., F.L.A.

Introduction

No-one can travel far in England without seeing an ancient parish church. The distant tower or spire of one may rise as a landmark; another, with neither, nestles modestly in a green churchyard. Our churches display a fascinating variety of shape, size, building materials and architectural style. Venture inside, and each is a surprise, apparently a law unto itself.

The eye is drawn, inevitably, to the east end, where light filtering through coloured glass illuminates the sanctuary, often with rich furnishings, suggesting peace, beauty, harmony, and a living order. An instinctive movement towards it is a symptom of the modern desire for easily acquired knowledge; but the craftsmen who built for worship to the glory of God never envisaged such a facile approach. Each part of the building was planned for a particular purpose and to convey special meaning. Comprehension comes from following these through with patience, beginning with the font near the door—farthest from the sanctuary—symbolising the entrance into Christian life through baptism.

Parish churches are functional buildings, expressing the needs and beliefs of local Christians at different periods. Each generation makes its own contribution; while changes imposed by authority are interpreted variously by individual bishops or parishes.

This brief account outlines the story of our English churches up to 1662, as they reflect the history of the worship for which they were intended.

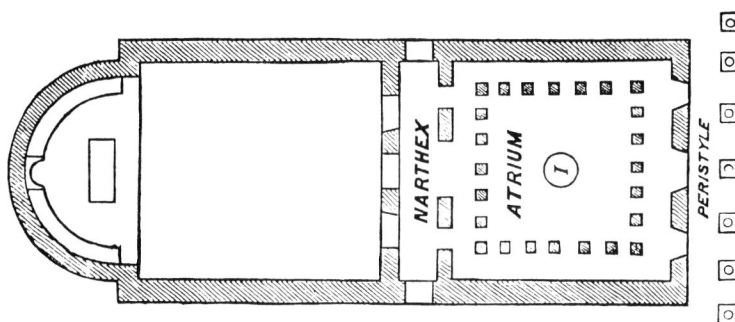

A Christian basilica, *or hall of a private Roman mansion developed into a church. In front is a peristyle, or row of columns, and an atrium or pillared courtyard, roofed over except above the central water-tank. Beyond, the narthex or ante-chamber leads into the basilica or hall, ending in a raised apse with its central table, reminiscent of the dining area of a Roman villa. This was approached by steps and separated by a balustrade.*

© Margot Johnson 1987
ISBN 0 946105 05 7

Cover picture: **Sidmouth Church, (Devon):** *engraving from a drawing by H. Hasler. Sidmouth Museum.*

THE FIRST ENGLISH PRAYER BOOK OF 1549

Henry VIII died in 1547/8 leaving parish churches, their clergy and religious beliefs almost unchanged. Yet Edward, his nine year old son and heir, had protestant tutors and a basically protestant Council of Regency was being planned.

Within a few months, Royal Injunctions prohibited pilgrimages to shrines, declaring health and grace derive from God only; commanded clergy to preach quarterly sermons against superstitions; forbade lights before statues and pictures, 'but only two lights upon the high altar before the Sacrament for the significance that Christ is the true light of the world'; ordered clergy to recite from the pulpit, on holy days when there was no sermon, the Lord's Prayer and Ten Commandments in English for people to learn by heart; and required clergy and clerks (choir) to say or sing the Litany in English, kneeling, before High Mass. Further Injunctions laid down times of daily services: Matins at 6 a.m. from Lady Day to 1 October, and in winter at 7 a.m.; Mass only once daily at 9 a.m.; and Evensong at 3 p.m. or 2 or 2.30 p.m. in winter. Images and pictures encouraging superstition must be removed; and no bells rung during Mass. Each church must have the *Paraphrases* (a commentary on the Gospels) and the *Homilies* (twelve sermons on the Scriptures, Justification by Faith, Good Works, etc.).

After a survey of church goods and numbers of communicants ('houseling people') in February 1547/8, sacring bells were confiscated.

Extreme protestants soon mocked the Mass itself, even corrupting Christ's words of institution, 'This is my body'. The Latin, *Hoc est corpus meum*, became 'hocus-pocus', a term meaning any superstitious nonsense. A new Act, however, penalised irreverence.

From 1547, the Epistle and Gospel must be read in English. While a committee of bishops worked on an English Mass, impatient congregations copied translations of the Sarum Use for themselves.

Henry VIII's Survey of Chantries made in 1546 was soon used to suppress them under a complicated Act. Their possessions were confiscated, and priests pensioned, chantry chapels becoming redundant; but chantry grammar schools were preserved. The Act was unpopular, for some chantries were endowed privately, while others belonged to guilds.

In 1548, an English *Order of Communion* appeared for use after the Consecration in the Latin Mass. It contained two long Exhortations to receive Communion (similar to the first and third in the 1662 Prayer Book); the short Exhortation ('Ye that do truly and earnestly repent you of your sins . . .'); the General Confession; Absolution; Comfortable Words; and the Prayer of Humble Access ('We do not presume to come to this thy table (O merciful lord) trusting in our own righteousness, but in thy manifold and great mercies . . .'); the Administration of both bread and wine to lay people (long denied them); and the Blessing. Afterwards the priest concluded with the Latin Post-Communion.

The First Prayer Book in English appeared in 1549. Its title, *The Booke of the Common Praier and Administration of the Sacraments and other Rites and Ceremonies of the Church after the Use of the Churche of England*, shows its purpose as a 'Use' based on ancient precedents.

The church was seen as the nation at prayer. Lay people, instead of being onlookers, were now expected to participate.

REFORMED USE OF MEDIEVAL CHURCHES

Medieval church builders lacked this concept of worship and the 1549 Prayer Book took for granted the division by a screen into chancel and nave and prescribed how these should now be used. The priest was to be 'in the quire (chancel)' for Matins and Evensong 'standing and turning him, so as he may best be heard of all such as be present'. In the Communion Service, while the clerks sang the Offertory sentences, the communicants were to move from nave to chancel, place their offerings in 'the poor men's box' (the 'strong chest' the 1547 Injunctions required to be placed near the high altar), and remain there, men on one side and women on the other, until the end of the service. Clergy and people worshipped together within the screen.

Extreme protestants thought the 1549 Book too compromising. Conservatives objected to its reforms. The section 'Of Ceremonies' makes its principles clear: 'it was thought expedient, not so much to have respect how to please and satisfy either of these parties, as how to please God, and to profit them both'.

In November 1550, bishops were ordered to command the removal of stone altars and their replacement by wooden tables (frequently like the contemporary domestic boards on frames or trestles).

Some clergy had already introduced tables as reminiscent of the Lord's Supper and following primitive examples, regarding stone altars in the context of Temple sacrifices superseded by Christ's 'once for all' sacrifice on Calvary. As they were moveable, a few clergy drew them from the east wall and celebrated facing west; many placed them lengthways in the chancel and communicants knelt round the table. The Sacrament was carried by the clergy to the people, who remained thus kneeling. Bishop Hooper argued (unsuccessfully) for the closure of chancels and holding all services in the nave.

Cranmer encouraged the reformer John Merbecke to simplify, from medieval plain-song, music for the Eucharist, Matins and Evensong suitable for congregational singing with 'as near as possible, for every syllable a note'. It appeared in 1550 in *The Booke of Common Praier noted*. Thomas Tallis (1505–85) wrote music for the Responses (still popular); and Christopher Tye (*c.* 1500–72) composed simple four-part anthems.

The Lord's Supper, *from an engraving in* A Course of Catechizing (*2nd edition, 1674*). *The altar is set table-wise in the chancel, a usual position for Communion until the Laudian reforms, and continued in some places after 1660. The celebrant stands at the north side (see the 1662 Prayer Book rubric) and the communicants kneel around. The Ten Commandments hang on the east wall.*

THE 1552 ENGLISH PRAYER BOOK

A second English Prayer Book followed in 1552. Chancels were to remain 'as in time past', but priestly functions, reference to auricular confession, and eucharistic vestments were now reformed. Prayers for the Dead were omitted. A General Confession and Absolution were made to introduce Morning and Evening Prayer, which had formerly begun with the Lord's Prayer. Baptism, which in 1549 retained exorcism, chrisom and unction, was simplified. The priest, in administering bread according to the 1549 Communion, said: 'The Body of our Lord Jesus Christ which was given for thee . . .'; in 1552, he must say instead: 'Take and eat this in remembrance that Christ died for thee . . .'.

To obtain uniformity of practice, the celebrant was to stand at the north side of the altar (now called the Holy Table), which it was perhaps assumed had its short ends east and west. It was to be placed for the Eucharist, by the church officers, wherever Matins and Evensong were taken. This, depending on audibility, might mean either chancel or nave, the former where there was a long chancel, the latter if it were small and enclosed. The Holy Table stood against the east wall except for Communion.

Queen Mary's Counter-Reformation

Edward VI's death in 1553 was disastrous to church reform. The Crown passed to Henry VIII's eldest daughter Mary, a half-Spaniard and fanatical Roman Catholic. Although discarding the title 'Supreme Head of the Church of England', she acted the part, aiming to destroy all her father's and brother's reforms. Reforming bishops were imprisoned (as were Cranmer, Latimer and Ridley from April 1554) or fled abroad, being replaced by men deprived for opposing Edward VI's reforms. Latin services were restored, stone altars rebuilt, old ways revived as far as possible, and a fifth of the clergy dismissed.

Most lay people, insufficiently understanding reformed doctrine after only four years of English services, accepted the situation; but when Mary married Philip of Spain in 1554, Spanish involvement, reunion with Rome, and restoration of church property in lay hands were prospects viewed with alarm.

The Pope·sent his legate, Reginald Pole (once Henry VIII's favourite); and Parliament rescinded all ecclesiastical legislation since 1528 except that dissolving the monasteries, so safeguarding lay financial interests; but trials for heresy soon followed and many were burnt at the stake for their faith, including Latimer and Ridley. In suffering this terrible death, Latimer cried to Ridley: 'Be of good comfort Master Ridley, and play the man; we shall this day light such a candle by God's grace in England as I trust shall never be put out'. Attempts to obtain Cranmer's recantation failed, and soon he suffered the same fate. That day Pole, ordained the previous day, said his first Mass and next day was consecrated Archbishop of Canterbury.

Soon, new monasteries were founded; and clergy married in Edward VI's reign had to choose between their wives and their livings. Philip, now King of Spain, quarrelled with a new Pope and dragged England into war with France. Continuing brutal persecution shocked all decent people.

Throughout the reign, English Prayer Book worship was maintained by exiles abroad; and a small congregation gathered secretly in various places in or near London, or on board a ship anchored in the Thames.

When Mary died in 1558 (and Cardinal Pole a few hours later) great rejoicing followed!

Reformation continued

THE CHURCH UNDER ELIZABETH I (1558–1603)

The new Queen began cautiously. Remaining parochial clergy were, officially, pro-Roman. Those deprived as Protestants favoured links with Geneva through returning exiles. Others preferred a middle course: a reformed catholic church free of both Rome and Geneva.

Elizabeth's first Parliament in 1559 made her 'Supreme Governor of church and state'; and imposed a new Prayer Book, almost that of 1552, but with a few changes. The words of administering the Sacrament combined those of the 1549 and 1552 Prayer Books; and the chalice was restored again to the laity. Under an *Ornaments Rubric* (so-named from directions in manuscripts in red), priests' eucharistic vestments must be those used in 2 Edward VI (i.e. in 1549)—a rule impossible to enforce; but ornaments re-introduced under Mary must be destroyed. Gradually, monthly Communions became normal.

Returning exiles, influenced by continental reformed worship, were scandalized by the compromise. Some, like William Whittingham (Calvin's relative by marriage), were ordained Presbyterians. Whittingham's English New Testament, published in Geneva in 1557, was the first to divide chapters into verses, following the example of Robert Étienne's Greek New Testament of 1551. (Chapters derive from manuscript divisions into sections for reading in church.) Whittingham and others, having begun the Geneva Bible in January 1558, delayed returning to England until its completion in 1560, dedicating it to Queen Elizabeth. Whittingham became Dean of Durham.

Bishops appointed under Mary refused to acknowledge Elizabeth; but Matthew Parker, member of the former Cambridge group studying Luther's teaching, became Archbishop of Canterbury, appointing moderate men under him. Taking a middle course, he fostered recognition of roots in the primitive church, through the Scriptures and good scholarship, an attitude later associated with 'Anglicanism'.

In 1560, Elizabeth ordered Parker to see that 'the tables of the Commandments be comely set or hung up in the east end of the chancel'; and in 1561 the exact place was identified as the wall above the Table. Often they remained from Edward VI's reign on the west side of the rood loft or above the chancel arch, staying there in spite of the order.

A Royal Order of 1561 commanded the removal of everything above the breast-summer (the load-bearing beam) of rood screens: crucifix, attendant figures, gallery and both parapets. Screens themselves must be retained (keeping chancels as formerly) being finished off with suitable coats of arms. The Royal Arms, popular in churches in Henry VIII's reign, was acceptable. Sometimes lay people had seats in the rood gallery, a practice continued in the 'flying pew' across the chancel arch. Examples survive at Whitby (North Yorkshire) in the Cholmley pew; and at Rycote Chapel (Oxfordshire).

Thomas Sternhold had published nineteen metrical Psalms in 1549 and John Hopkins and others completed the whole Psalter in metre, issuing it for church use in 1562. Although in poor verse, it achieved great popularity among the unlettered, who could learn simple hymns.

Clergy who found preaching difficult welcomed the Second Book of Homilies published the same year. Bishops tried to educate them, bidding them acquire Bibles, the *Paraphrases* (commentaries) and note-books. To remedy a clergy shortage, the order of Reader was revived temporarily. Education in general was improving. New grammar schools were founded, some teaching music; and at Oxford and Cambridge the collegiate system expanded to include students formerly living in lodgings.

From 1571 Puritan clergy, seeking to transform the church peacefully, formed voluntary groups throughout England, holding outside church time free types of service with preaching. Through the 'classis' system, local clergy committees chose ordination candidates, privately ordained them, and sent them to the bishop for episcopal ordination. They wanted lay power increased and church government by assemblies and church sessions instead of bishops, objecting to ornaments and vestments (even the surplice), organs, and musical instruments in church, among other things. Some bishops encouraged their activities as doing much good; but Elizabeth disapproved, fearing Prayer Book worship and the established church would be undermined.

Elizabeth's policy of toleration became upset by foreign interference in support of the pro-Roman party's determination to overthrow the English church.

In 1568, William Allen, an English recusant, founded a college at Douai to train for England missionaries prepared to die—an idea copied elsewhere.

By 1580, about a hundred Roman priests had arrived; while the Pope encouraged plots to assassinate Elizabeth. She, in self-defence, had the priests sought out where possible and executed. Fines were imposed in 1581 for absence from church; and when the Throckmorton Plot against her life was uncovered in 1583, all Jesuit and seminary priests were ordered to leave. Plots continued and in 1587 Mary, Queen of Scots, was executed for fomenting disobedience. Roman Catholics became increasingly identified with Spanish and papal politics.

A papal military crusade against England was planned from 1585, culminating in 1588 in the Spanish Armada. After its defeat, foreign support for English Romanists ceased. They were ordered to return to their places of origin, not moving more than five miles away. About 250 refused to comply and were executed.

Elizabeth's *Via Media*, her 'middle way', was at last secure.

EARLY SEVENTEENTH-CENTURY CHURCHMANSHIP

On Elizabeth's death in 1603, her successor was her cousin, James I, son of Mary, Queen of Scots, who became James VI of Scotland at a few months old on his mother's abdication in 1567.

Flamborough (St. Oswald), *North Humberside: the fine fifteenth-century rood loft, by the Ripon school of woodcarvers, still retains some of its original colours: black, crimson, blue and gold. Later used as a west gallery, it once had fifteen niches, two being lost at the left end during restoration. Above the chancel arch hangs the Belief, i.e. the Creed, Ten Commandments, and Lord's Prayer.*

Walter Scott (Bradford) Ltd.

Elizabeth's tolerance had left great diversity in arrangements for worship; and the Puritan party, believing John Knox and the Scottish reformers had influenced James, promptly met him, hoping to revive their cause.

A conference at Hampton Court in 1604 heard their demands; but the King, who presided, made it clear they must suffer penalties or conform to the Prayer Book, to which minor additions were now made, including the end of the Catechism. A new translation of the Bible was proposed, appearing in 1611 as the Authorized Version, dedicated to James I.

After the conference, many Puritans fled to Holland; but a group returned from Leyden in 1620 to organise a party of emigrants. They sailed in the *Mayflower* from Plymouth to Massachusetts, founding a colony based on their religious and political principles.

A survey in 1603 numbered 8,500 recusants and James, although mistrusting them, declared amity; Romanist seminary priests grasped the opportunity to return in strength, but the Gunpowder Plot, engineered by fanatics in 1605, increased popular dislike of recusants. They must now not only attend English services, but receive Holy Communion. A special service of thanksgiving for deliverance from the plot was added to the Prayer Book.

James' proposal to marry Prince Charles to a Spanish princess, accompanied by concessions to English Roman Catholics, was unsuccessful, but led to suspicions of both King and court.

James, however, was not pro-Roman. Convinced of the Divine Right of Kings, and believing monarchy and episcopacy to be complementary, he supported the established Church of England.

ANGLICANISM AND CHARLES I

Richard Bancroft was an able Archbishop of Canterbury (1604–10) but his successor, George Abbot (1610–32), alienated inadvertently both Puritans and High Churchmen.

When James I died in March 1625, his son Charles I succeeded him. Convinced by upbringing of the Divine Right of Kings, he considered himself above the law. Parliament, however, seeing its duties other than in financing royal despotism, sought to prevent his intervention in church affairs; but Charles dissolved Parliament and ruled for eleven years by Royal Prerogative, entrusting affairs of state to the Earl of Strafford and ecclesiastical matters to William Laud (Bishop of London from 1628, and Archbishop of Canterbury from 1633).

Laud held high ideals about dignity and order, but mercilessly enforced rigid discipline through the Court of High Commission. Puritans were treated cruelly, some being pilloried or having their ears cut off.

In 1617, as Dean of Gloucester, he had persuaded the Chapter to replace the Communion Table permanently at the east end of the choir on the uppermost step to prevent abuse. Ornately carved Elizabethan Tables were too heavy to move regularly, as intended, from where they stood for Communion to the east wall. Consequently in some places, through slackness, they were used for teaching children, making up churchwardens' accounts, or even for holding hats and cloaks. The Gloucester arrangement was copied elsewhere, but as it did not succeed entirely, Laud and his supporters advocated rails, so introducing the practice of going up to receive Communion. Rails were not new, being known occasionally on the Continent and in a few English churches under Elizabeth I. Laud insisted that the position of the Communion Table was theologically unimportant and should be left to the local bishop's discretion.

The piety, devotion and writings of some contemporary scholars had lasting influence. A new interest in the Greek Fathers and the history of liturgy led to the desire to improve church interiors and the conduct of worship, and to raise educational and moral standards among parish clergy, who varied between slovenly and excellent.

Among the best was George Herbert (1593–1633), whose poems on the church appeared as *The Temple*. His prose *A Priest in the Temple* describes his ideal for a country parson. He 're-edified' and refurnished his church at Leighton Bromswold (Huntingdonshire) from 1627, installing, on either side of the chancel arch, pulpits for reading the service and preaching, that 'they should neither have a precedence or priority of the other; but that prayer and preaching, being equally useful, might agree like brothers, and have an equal honour and estimation'. This famous remark differs slightly from Ferrar's explanation (see below). Herbert advocated an hour-long sermon, fairly short at a time when some lasted three hours. Similar twin pulpits, reminiscent of early ambos, were copied widely, perhaps a reaction from the high pulpit with reading desk attached below.

Nicholas Ferrar (1593–1637), brought up in business with the Virginia Company, formed the idea of a family-based religious community. Leaving London in 1626, he moved to the Manor House, Little Gidding (Huntingdonshire), with his mother, brother and sister-in-law with their three children, his sister with her husband and sixteen children, and their servants.

Ferrar's description of ordering the church that year says: 'the pulpit was fixed on the north, and the reading desk over against it on the south side of the church, and both on the same level, it being thought improper that a higher place should be appointed for preaching than that which was allotted for prayer'. Ferrar provided 'a pillar and eagle of brass for the Bible' beside the reading desk. Only a step divided nave from chancel. On the east wall he erected three brass tablets engraved with the Decalogue, Creed, and Lord's Prayer. The altar stood table-wise, with green coverings for everyday use, and a rich blue cloth, with lace and a silver fringe, for festivals. Upon it stood wax candles in silver candlesticks.

The family rose daily at 4 a.m., said the first Office at 6 a.m., and repeated the Offices during the day until the last at 9 p.m. In addition they kept a Night Watch in turns, repeating the whole Psalter, kneeling. During the remaining hours they educated their own and local children, helped the sick and poor, composed Gospel Harmonies (concordances) and held the so-called 'Little Academy' for study and discussion.

After Nicholas Ferrar died in 1637, the community continued. A Puritan book of 1641 attacked it; and in 1646, in the Civil War, Little Gidding was sacked, and many of its treasures burnt. The family escaped, and some of the Ferrar manuscripts survive, recording much about contemporary ideals of worship.

John Cosin (1594–1672), scholar, historian and liturgiologist, became rector of Brancepeth, County Durham, refurbishing its church magnificently. His chancel screen and stalls are crowned with fine tabernacle work. Above the eastern bay is the best surviving example of a ceiling designed to enhance the dignity of the altar beneath, in the absence of a tester (a type of canopy): angels carry shields bearing Latin inscriptions praising God. The bench ends are tall poppy-heads; and the pinnacled font cover is surmounted by a flying angel. All recalls the best medieval style. Cosin became Dean of Peterborough and sought refuge in Paris during the Civil War. At the Restoration in 1660, he returned to become Bishop of Durham and influenced the 1662 Book of Common Prayer.

Haughton-le-Skerne (St. Andrew), *County Durham: a Norman church, with panelled walls and furnishings typical of the 1630s (although said to be of 1662). In the chancel are communicants' stalls; a 'low-side window'; and, formerly, a narrow canopy over the altar. In the nave are twin pulpits, for reading the service and preaching, flanking the low Norman chancel arch; matching box pews with panelled doors, bench ends rusticated below, with strap-work higher up, and crowned by poppy-heads; canopied churchwardens' seats; a similar canopy over the south door; a font cover of c. 1662; and Saxon sculptured fragments assembled on the north wall. The church is seen decorated for Easter.*

Gordon Coates

Abbey Dore, *Herefordshire: the chancel screen of 1634, showing Renaissance influence, bears three coats of arms, with the Stuart royal arms over the central opening. In the original arrangement (since changed) the chancel was left empty for Communion services; the old stone **mensa** was re-fixed on stone columns for use as an altar; and the pews, west gallery and pulpit with tester were all placed west of the screen. At the Dissolution, the Cistercian abbey passed to the Scudamore family; and in 1633 John, 1st Viscount Scudamore, gave to the parishioners the choir and transepts, which were largely re-built and re-furnished at his expense under the architect and military engineer John Abel (1577–1674). The nave was demolished and a tower built over the angle of the south transept.*
Roger Dauncey

Meantime, Charles determined to reform the Scottish Kirk, which was established on Calvinist-Presbyterian principles. In 1629 Laud, assisted by John Maxwell (later Bishop of Ross), began preparations for a Scottish Prayer Book. Known in advance as 'Laud's Liturgy', cries of 'The Mass is entered amongst us' and riotous scenes greeted its introduction to St. Giles, Edinburgh, in 1637, for Laud was suspected of being a secret papist. The consequence was the Covenant, signed by most Scottish people against anything imperilling the Kirk. In 1639, the General Assembly resolved to abolish both episcopacy and the Prayer Book; and war with England followed. When Charles had to recall both Houses of Parliament to obtain funds in 1640, Convocation took steps to strengthen connections between monarch and church, uphold episcopal government, and restore altars to their old places in churches.

The situation now worsened. Parliament, recalled in August that year, impeached the Earl of Strafford, who was executed; the 'Root and Branch' petition of 15,000 Londoners demanded abolition of episcopal government as fostering 'Romish superstitions'; and Laud was impeached and imprisoned. 'The Grand Remonstrance' presented grievances against the King in December 1641, but failed; and in January 1642 Charles left London, setting up his standard in Nottingham in August.

The Church in the Civil War and Commonwealth

The war was fought between Charles, claiming the 'Divine Right of Kings' and representing episcopacy and the Prayer Book; and Parliament, standing for Puritanism, both Presbyterian and Independent. The former relied on autocracy and despotism, the latter wanted civil liberty. Both sides found Scriptural justification for their cause. The fighting caused great destruction and Puritans attacked churches and church property, breaking stained glass, burning books and vestments, and destroying furnishings.

The Westminster Assembly of Divines, set up by Parliament, drew up in 1643 the *Solemn League and Covenant* for 'the extirpation of popery, prelacy, superstition, heresy, schism, profaneness, and whatsoever shall be found contrary to sound doctrine . . .' while intending to 'preserve the rights and privileges of the Parliament and the liberties of the Kingdoms' without diminishing 'His Majesty's just power and greatness'. This was imposed on all males over eighteen when it became law in February 1644. As 'prelacy' was defined to include bishops and all church-officers depending on episcopacy, it meant the end of the Church of England wherever Parliament ruled. Over 2,000 clergy were evicted, their wives and children being allowed one-fifth of the value of their benefices as a pension (seldom paid). Some went abroad; others obtained tutor's or chaplain's posts; a number were imprisoned; the remainder continued as Presbyterian or Independent ministers.

In January 1645 Archbishop Laud was executed. A few days earlier the Book of Common Prayer was declared illegal, being replaced by the *Directory of Public Worship* which called it 'an offence' and laid down rules for Baptisms, the Lord's Supper, the Solemnization of Matrimony, the Visitation of the Sick, and the Burial of the Dead. It gave no forms of prayer, not even the Lord's Prayer. Among other things it abolished were the sign of the cross in baptism, godparents, the ring in marriage, and any religious observance at burial. The Communion Table was to be brought from the chancel into the nave, and the Sacrament received sitting or standing.

Soon, England was divided into *classes* for Presbyterian church government by provincial and national assemblies, but as Milton said: 'New Presbyter is but old Priest writ large'. A new tyranny emerged, driving many to transfer their allegiance to the rising 'Independents', who included Oliver Cromwell.

The Royalists were defeated by his New Model Army at Naseby in 1645, but Parliament proved intolerant of all except Presbyterians. In June 1647, the observance of Easter, Whit Sunday and Christmas was prohibited. Some clergy continued to minister to faithful lay people by using Prayer Book services either in church or secretly in houses, sometimes altering them sufficiently to keep within the law while maintaining their character. In

December 1647, the House of Commons received complaints of 'Malignant ministers' using the Prayer Book in some parts of London; but at Christmas St. Martin-in-the-Fields and St. Margaret's, Westminster, rebelled. Rioting broke out at Ealing and Canterbury. Ordinary people objected greatly to the prohibitions relating to baptism, marriage (now a civil contract before a J.P.) and burial, many seeking an ordained minister privately.

Meantime intrigues and discussions involving Charles I persisted, and he might have made an advantageous peace as his opponents were divided. Instead, he sought Scottish help in return for establishing Presbyterianism in England for three years, greatly incensing the Independents.

War broke out again, this time with parliamentary support for the King; but Cromwell and his army were victorious. The House of Commons was purged of all likely opponents and Charles was brought before it, tried, and executed on 30 January, 1649.

At his burial at St. George's chapel, on 9 February, the Bishop of London (who had attended him on the scaffold) used the Prayer Book, but the Governor of Windsor Castle stopped the service.

Horror at the beheading, and Charles' dignified bearing at the end, gained him much sympathy; while the subsequent military despotism proved worse than the King's autocracy.

From 1662 to 1859, Charles I's execution was commemorated in the Prayer Book calendar by special services. He had become a martyr for creed and church.

Cromwell's ambiguous *Instrument of Government* of 1653 allowed people to worship as they chose and many independent sects arose; but toleration was not extended to Anglicans or Roman Catholics. From January 1656 severe penalties were laid on all who used the Prayer Book; but in November 1657 Cromwell's daughter Mary, with her father's connivance, was privately married at Hampton Court, using the Prayer Book rite. The Cromwell women had remained faithful Anglicans!

Cromwell died in 1658. He was succeeded as Protector by his son Richard, who resigned in 1660.

The Restoration and the 1662 Book of Common Prayer

The army, led by General Monck, dissolved the Rump Parliament and arranged for an election. The new Parliament invited Charles II to return from exile in Holland as King. He arrived amid great rejoicing, having published in advance the *Declaration of Breda* offering a general pardon and religious toleration in response to a Puritan

delegation, promising them a conference. As Charles favoured Anglicans, those in exile returned. Angicans received cathedral appointments and elected bishops of similar views. Parliament proved to be predominantly Anglican also, its members often being former pupils of tutors who were clergy deprived in the Commonwealth.

The promised conference met at the Savoy Hospital on 15 August, 1661. Twelve bishops and twelve Puritan divines attended, each side with nine assistants. Archbishop Gilbert Sheldon presided, taking Prayer Book restoration for granted. Richard Baxter, one of the century's best theologians, led the Puritan side, believing the Prayer Book 'a true worship but imperfect'. He thought all but one of his associates held the same view. His printed objections were long and detailed. They included use of the surplice, the sign of the cross in Baptism and kneeling at Communion; while requesting extempore prayer, making the Litany continuous by removing the responses, renaming Sunday the Lord's Day, and calling priests minsters. As a result, Prayer Book revision was proposed.

Eight bishops, commissioned with the revision, met in November 1661. Among them were Robert Sanderson, who took part in discussions for revision in 1641; Matthew Wren, who vetted the ill-fated 1637 Scottish Prayer Book; John Cosin, who brought long-prepared proposals and acted as secretary; and his successor in this office, William Sancroft, later Archbishop of Canterbury.

A desire to restore the 1549 Communion Service was rejected lest it upset the Puritans; but the Black Rubric of 1552 was restored. It says of the order to kneel at Communion: 'it is not meant thereby that any adoration is done or ought to be done, either unto the Sacramental bread and wine there bodily received, or to any essential presence there being of Christ's natural flesh and blood'. The words 'real and essential presence' were altered to 'real and corporal presence'.

In all, about 600 alterations were made—mostly small—including rules for the manual acts in the Prayer of Consecration, the remembrance of the dead in the Prayer for the Church Militant, and some use of the word 'minister' for 'priest'. All passages from the Bible, except the Canticles and Psalms, were to be from the Authorized Version, prayers were added from the 1637 Scottish Prayer Book, and other new prayers included the General Thanksgiving. A form of 'Baptism for those of Riper Years' provided for those who had grown up unbaptised during the Commonwealth and for converts 'in our plantations', a reference to the American colonies.

The revisers sought, by returning to ancient precedents, to re-establish Anglican worship rooted in Scripture and free from medieval accretions, superstition and mis-interpretation. Their new additions to meet contemporary needs followed the style of Cranmer's incomparable English in translating from his sources, keeping faithful to the tradition of a special language of worship originating in the first-century synagogue. Many of its easily memorable phrases soon passed into

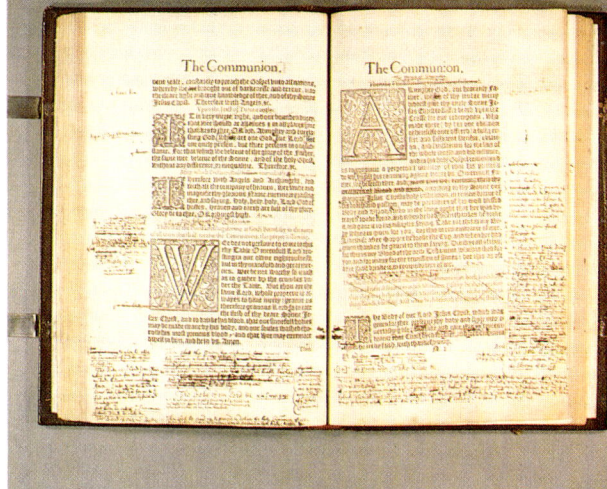

The Book of Common Prayer: *the folio edition of 1619, annotated in Bishop John Cosin's own hand in making the first draft of the revision of the* Book of Common Prayer *in 1661. The opening shows the Prayer of Humble Access; the Consecration; and the beginning of the Administration. Cosin's Library, in the handsome room he built as a public library, still retains its identity within Durham University Library which administers it.* Durham University Library (Cosin D.III.5)

everyday usage, teaching, edifying and constantly reminding of the Christian basis of life.

The Prayer Book was intended to become 'Common' to clergy and laity alike, embracing everything necessary for daily prayer and Bible reading as well as for Sunday worship, besides providing for all the major events of life from the cradle to the grave. It was envisaged as the framework of an everyday life of devotion for ordinary people.

It was imposed by an Act of Uniformity ordering its use by clergy and school-masters from St. Bartholomew's Day (24 August) 1662. Those refusing were deprived.

Subsequent legislation, relaxed later in the century, forbade participation in any form of worship apart from the established church. This led to a new era of religious divisions which cut across England's entire social structure, but many non-conformists came to base their service on the Book of Common Prayer, quoting extensively from its prayers.

The story of how the Prayer Book was intended to be used, and how Anglican worship affected the development of our ancient churches and the styles of new ones over the next 300 years, must be told in a separate booklet.

In recent years, experimental services were published as a separate series, now discontinued; and in 1980, new variant forms appeared in the Alternative Service Book, authorised for use until the year 2000.

The Book of Common Prayer of 1662, however, still remains the official Prayer Book of the Church of England.

Winchcombe (St. Peter), *Gloucestershire: rebuilt in 1460 on a new site at the west end of the Benedictine abbey which, as rector, paid for the chancel. The parishioners collected £200 for the nave, their responsibility, and Ralph Boteler, Lord Sudeley, met the remaining cost. The chancel, partly rebuilt in 1690, has triple sedilia (?fourteenth century) separated by image niches, all with crocketed canopies. The piscina has a stone tabernacle above with the arms of Winchcombe Abbey, Gloucester Abbey, and Sir Ralph Boteler, and a heart beneath. There are fifteenth-century screens from former chantry chapels; a balustrade alms box, c. 1547, with three locks for the imcumbent and two churchwardens; an organ case of c. 1735, reputedly by Grinling Gibbons; and a Flemish brass candelabra, given in 1753. The east window of 1866 shows a ship in sail. An ornate stone reredos of 1876, a flight of steps to the altar, encaustic tiles, and a brass rail are part of the restoration of 1872–6 in the supposed 'correct' medieval style.*

***Below:** Before 1660 and until 1872, the altar was railed on the west and had wainscot on the other three sides. In the re-ordering of 1872, only the altar table was kept. The photograph of c. 1870 shows the altar cloth in use until 1872, and now displayed on the wall of the north aisle. It was made from two disused priests' copes of c. 1382 by Katharine of Aragon and her ladies, probably when she and Henry VIII were at Sudeley Castle (then a royal residence) from July to September 1535. Her pomegranate badge alternates with a pansy on the border. The body of Christ, missing from the cross, is incorporated into another work from Katharine's needle at Minsterworth, Gloucestershire (see page 20).*